CHORLEY
AND DISTRICT

Chorley's first Town Hall was built in 1802 on the corner of Union Street and Market Street. The bell hammer was called 'Th'owd Tup' as it was shaped like a ram's head.

Britain in Old Photographs

Chorley
and District

Jack Smith

Market Street in the 1920s, with St Mary's girls in a Walk of Witness, usually just called Walking Day. To the right is the White Bull, with the Cunliffe Arms to the centre left.

First published 1994
This edition published 2009
Reprinted 2023

The History Press
97 St George's Place,
Cheltenham, Gloucestershire, GL50 3QB
www.thehistorypress.co.uk

© Jack Smith, 1994, 2009

The right of Jack Smith to be identified as the Author
of this work has been asserted in accordance with the
Copyrights, Designs and Patents Act 1988.

All rights reserved. No part of this book may be reprinted
or reproduced or utilised in any form or by any electronic,
mechanical or other means, now known or hereafter invented,
including photocopying and recording, or in any information
storage or retrieval system, without the permission in writing
from the Publishers.
British Library Cataloguing in Publication Data.
A catalogue record for this book is available from the British Library.

ISBN 978 0 7524 4948 7

Typesetting and origination by
The History Press
Printed by TJ Books Limited, Padstow, Cornwall

CONTENTS

	Introduction	6
1.	Chorley, Town and Outskirts	9
2.	Lowland Villages	59
3.	Hill Country	95
	Acknowledgements	128

Church School reunion, 1925. In the centre of the second row, wearing a hat, is Mrs Ritson, wife of the former Rivington Church vicar.

INTRODUCTION

Having had a life-long interest in local history, from prehistoric times to the present, it was always envisaged that I would set down some of my findings in book form. Although a book of photographs was not intended as a first, during the period researching this book I have learned a great deal more than I thought I knew. Moving around the 80 square miles of rural Chorley, visiting everything from villages to demolition sites, playing detective to trace a family or a former occupation, I have met a great number of people, have drunk copious cups of tea, and have heard so many stories and anecdotes concerning the area that I could have filled a book twice the size of this – let alone using any photographs.

By being 'out in the field', the social and industrial history of the recent past has 'come to life', so to speak. I have discussed with people approaching their ninetieth year how it was to work 'part time,' or how they had to walk for miles to get to their place of work. To me it has all been Chorley, not a particular parish or village; if there is to be any criticism then it is only that too many of the parishes in the district are extremely parochial. Some of them are more insular than others, hardly knowing where another parish is, at the opposite side of the district. Having now set down in one book a little about each of the twenty-three parishes that make up Chorley as a whole, I have attained my goal and, I hope, created more of an awareness among all the townships about the district. This 'heart of Lancashire' countryside has a great wealth of natural history, of beautiful places to visit, as well as character and individuality.

Chorley is located on the eastern edge of the Lancashire Plain, which extends to the Irish Sea coast 20 miles to the west. On the east side of the town are the foothills of the Pennines, rising as high moorland up to 1,200 feet. The hills give the town protection from the east winds and snow. Many rivers flow through the district, all rising in the hills, and many of the early industries began along them. To the south-west lies the former Lancashire coalfield. With Chorley being on the edge of this, pits were dug in the town and in some of the villages. Sadly no pits remain today and the buildings around them have been cleared away, the sites becoming today the province of the industrial historian.

Founded in Saxon times Chorley has developed around its church, which during that time was a small chapel located on a hill overlooking the valley of the River Chor. The area was called the 'ley' by the Chor; hence Chorley. By about 1810 that original small community had grown to 5,000 persons, the Lancaster to Wigan Canal had been built through the town, and all the streets had been named and numbered. Some steam-driven mills had even been built. In 1811 Chorley Workhouse had its first school, and in 1815, after the Napoleonic Wars, a report said that Chorley had '302 families or 3,307 persons in the town who are poor' – about half of the population.

Chorley Town Hall, built in 1879, with adjoining buildings decorated for some special occasion, possibly the coronation of King George V.

With the coming of the Leeds to Liverpool Canal in 1816, in addition to the trade already created with the Lancaster Canal, Botany Bay, Chorley's 'port', became a busy place and a community developed around it. In 1820 gas lamps were first used in the town, and two years later Park Road was built. In the 1840s a sewage system was installed and the railway arrived.

By 1901, when Chorley's population had risen to 26,852, great changes had occurred in transportation, communication and methods of production, all having come from the so-called 'Industrial Revolution'. Changes to the countryside were created by the need for more stone and coal, the construction of railways, canals, mills and associated housing. The infrastructure of the town and village saw great changes too, with road alterations, piped water, gas and sewage schemes. In Chorley 6,000 persons were working in cotton mills, some 17,900 looms and 500,000 spindles were in use, and a further three mills were about to be built: Cowling Mill in 1906, Talbot Mill in 1910 and Park Mill in 1914. The need for more iron led to the setting up of several foundries in and around the area; some of these produced machine parts, lamp-posts, fireplaces, grids and cast-iron columns for mill construction.

At the outbreak of the First World War there were thirty cotton manufacturers in the town. Shops and businesses thrived in town and country, ranging from coopers, hay, straw and provender dealers to lath renders and squeezer-makers. The Chorley Co-operative Society Ltd, which had started in 1887, now had twelve shops in the area. As yet there was no public park, but there was a slaughter-house and a library. The biggest change to occur in the area, after the war and the advent of electricity in 1923, was in the 1930s. The coronation year of 1937 is a good milestone to discuss change. In that year 2,000 acres of land in Euxton were purchased by the Ministry of Defence in order to build a Royal Ordnance Factory. During the Second World War over 40,000 persons were employed at the munitions site. Hostels had been built to accommodate many of these people; three were built locally, one in Chorley and two in Euxton. A large number of employees at the factory, from towns all over the county, were brought by train and bus. During those dark days of the war the ROF at Chorley was frequently mentioned by the ubiquitous 'Germany Calling' radio network, whose English-speaking 'Lord Haw Haw' had visited Chorley in the mid-1930s.

The 1950s and '60s saw much of the old town of Chorley greatly altered, with many of its stone-built terraced rows swept away to be replaced by council houses, which encroached into the countryside. Farms on the edge of town were now engulfed and open fields gave way to roads. Although the character of the town and its villages survived, many of the old buildings of historical importance were lost during this time, such as Duxbury Hall and handloom weavers' cottages. The early 1970s saw the proposals outlined for a 'new town', which would encompass Preston, Leyland and Chorley and would include more housing developments, new road systems, complete new villages and the like. It was after these proposals, in about 1974, that the Walton Summit branch of the Lancaster Canal was filled in. However, the Central Lancashire Development Corporation and all its proposals eventually went away, but not before the whole of the district had been subjected to major alterations. Fortunately the landscaping carried out then has grown to cover the scars left by the massive changes.

The 1990s saw Chorley's first shopping precinct 'Market Walk' created and a pedestrianised zone around the covered market area. The 1960s bus station was demolished in the new millennium, and a new bus station built close to the railway station. The town centre bypass road was opened, being a diverted A6, leading to development changes along its route.

The town continues to expand, and a new village is being built on the site of the former Royal Ordnance Factory, which ceased production at the end of 2007. It is called Buckshaw Village. In 2003, Talbot Mill weaving shed closed and was subsequently demolished. Late 2008 has seen the last spinning and weaving carried out in the town, with the closure of the Messrs Lawrence's. The end of an era, for Chorley was once one of Lancashire's cotton towns.

Today Chorley is still a market town, as it has been for 500 years, its 'flat iron' market still keeping a precarious hold of its site despite its reduction for car parking. After all, the markets are an essential part of Chorley's character and history, as well as providing a social and practical retail outlet.

Jack Smith
February 2008

SECTION ONE

CHORLEY, TOWN AND OUTSKIRTS

'Greetings from Chorley': a postcard from the early 1900s showing four different views around the town.

Chorley's oldest building is the parish church of St Lawrence. The church was first mentioned in the fourteenth century, but it is likely that a small church would have been here in Saxon times. Connected with most of the local families over the centuries, it is best known for its association with the Standish family; a branch of this family lived at Duxbury Hall. It may be that Myles Standish, who sailed with the Pilgrim Fathers from Plymouth in 1620, was born here. During the 1940s, when the USAAF were encamped in Chorley, the possible connection with their country's founding and Myles Standish was commemorated with the presentation of a flag, which still hangs over the Standish family pew.

Chorley parish church Walking Day in the early 1900s. The children with their 'escorts' were photographed in Parker Street.

The parish church had two schools, one for girls and the other for boys. Both had playgrounds, but no field until one was purchased some years later. This photograph shows the official opening of the field in about 1920.

A display float used by the gasworks and other trades at the Town Hall opening day celebrations, 1879. Gas was first used for street lighting in Chorley in 1819, when excess gas for Timothy Lightoller's mill in Standish Street was used to illuminate the street itself. In the 1830s, when the population had risen to about 7,500, a gasworks was built to satisfy increased demand.

An organ grinder in Chapel Street, near the corner of New Market Street, early 1900s. The Victoria Arms pub and the then popular 'Unter dem Linden' Café can be seen in the background.

A game of bowls, 1890s. This was obviously serious stuff by the looks on their faces. On the right is Mr Taylor, who worked at the Chorley Wagon Works.

Trades' procession, 1890s. Viewed along New Market Street towards Chapel Street is a procession of horse-drawn wagons, floats and such like, some of which are carrying advertisements. To the left are swingboats and an ice-cream seller. The large building to the centre and left is Mr Testo Sante's Grand Theatre, which was burned down in 1914. After the fire Mr Sante set up his theatre in the Drill Hall of the local Artillery Company in Salisbury Street, which is off Cunliffe Street.

A large gathering at 'Flat Iron' market-place, pre-1914. This glass plate view of the market area may show a religious gathering as the banners on the side of Sante's Theatre are from churches, one of these being Trinity Methodist.

Walking Day, pre-1914. Strangely enough the banner behind the children is also from Trinity Church. Perhaps it is the same event as the top photograph since the parade is passing the front of Sante's.

Delivering beer from Whittle Springs Brewery to the Fazackerley Arms pub (recently demolished), *c.* 1900. The brewery claimed to use water from the famous Whittle Springs spa, ensuring its goodness.

A horse and cart from Birkacre, 1920s. The decorated horses and cart are taking part in some sort of procession in Park Road.

Royal Albert pub, Market Street, 1890. Standing at the door is the landlord Mr Gillet. He had a large family, mainly of sons who played in a band at the pub.

Another old Chorley pub, early 1900s. This is the Britannia, which was located in Water Street on the old coach road. Peter O'Malia, the landlord, is standing at the door.

Preston Road, Chorley, showing the local fishmonger selling from his cart, 1892. In the 1890s Chorley had six fishmongers, more than there are today. The cottages in the background date from the late eighteenth century. The larger building to the end of the row was formerly the Toll Gate cottage for traffic entering the town from the north.

Anderton Street, decorated for Queen Victoria's Diamond Jubilee, 1897. Processions and extra gas lighting were also a feature of the celebrations.

Pall Mall Arch, 1911. In common with many other towns was the building of decorative arches for special occasions. Built of wood by local groups, this one was built for the coronation of King George V.

Market Street, looking north. Before the days of the motor vehicle the main traffic through town was horse and cart. The cart in the foreground is loading furniture.

St Thomas's Road. To the left is Crown Street with the old police station beyond. At the corner of Crown Street was the police superintendent's house and offices.

Chorley railway station was sited in Railway Street in 1842 when the railway first came to town. In the 1880s the station was resited and a bridge built for pedestrians to cross the tracks. However, many avoided using this and were run over.

Chapel Street, pre-1913. Many of the shop-fronts have changed little until recent times. To the left is Leach's, a large furniture shop complete with hoist to raise items of furniture to the upstairs showroom.

St Thomas's Square, 1888. St Mary's Ladies' Cycle Club is preparing to leave on an excursion. Behind the ladies can be seen the property in Mealhouse Lane, which was demolished before the building of the White Hart.

The ladies are now passing the old entrance gate to Astley Park on their way to their soirée, possibly to Whittle Springs some 3 miles away, which at that time was a spa where a hotel had been built.

Market Place, c. 1910. Viewed from the end of Hill Street the market stalls look about the same as they do today, although the fashions have certainly changed.

The market again. During the 1920s one of the most popular stalls, especially with the children, was that of Midgeley's. This photograph shows the stall's selection of sweets: 'Boiled Sweets . . . 4d a pound'.

St George's Church was built in 1825, but it was almost a hundred years later when it acquired a clock. The church was built using some of the £1 million allocated by the government for new churches.

Edward Lawrence. The cotton business of Messrs Lawrence & Sons was established in the 1850s. Edward came of age in 1899 and a booklet of photographs was produced by local photographer Luke Berry. The book shows decorations at the factory (see opposite).Although the name of Lawrence's was retained, new owners ran the mill from c.1970s. During this period, cotton goods manufacture gave way to the use of man-made fibre yarns, with the installation of specialist machinery. Including 'state of the art' Swiss looms. (One Lancashire Loom was retained for a special contract only, until 2006).

The mills continued until late 2008, when the business was closed. As the very last such mill in the town, its many processes were recorded on photograph by the author. He was also given the last shuttle used on the very last Lancashire Loom to work in Chorley.

Some of the decorations inside the factory 'shed'. In addition to these there was a great amount of decoration outside the factory as well.

The upper photograph dates from about 1900 and shows Market Street with its shop canopies, noticeably without cars. The photograph below may well have been taken twenty-five or more years later. At that time you could obviously stop to collect your shopping leaving the car parked outside.

No, this is not a still from a silent movie, but Chorley's first self-propelled fire engine in the early 1920s. The vehicle was a Leyland and may have been built at the Grime Street mill, Chorley. Previously two horse-drawn steam-pumps, called Albany and Bobs, served the town.

Looking out of the window of Mr Harrison's shop in Bolton Road, across to the former handloom weavers' cottages opposite. Mr Harrison is unloading goods from his car.

On Thursday the 8th.
A FOOT RACE
For Half-a-Guinea, or a New Pair of Shoes,

By men in wooden Clogs, from opposite the Royal Oak and Bull's Head, to the Joiner's Arms and back; each clog to contain six pease.—N. B, The pease to be counted upon their return, and no boiling allowed.

Also Seven Shillings

To be jumped for, by men in sacks, from the above place, to the Fish Stones and back; the second best to have 2s. 6d.—N. B. Coal Sacks will be preferred, and no jockeying allowed. The Candidates to provide their own Sacks.

Also, seven Shillings

To be run for, by men with wooden Legs, from the above place, to the Joiner's Arms and back; the second best to be entitled to 2s. 6d.—N. B. If any accident arises in the contest from fracture, a new leg will be provided.

A POUND OF SNUFF

To be run for by old women, not less than 40 years of age, from the above place, to the Joiner's Arms and back; second best to have four ounces.

To enter each Day at Ten o'Clock, and Start precisely at One.

This is the lower half of an 1814 poster advertising Chorley Races (the top half refers to conventional horse-racing on Monday, Tuesday and Wednesday). But how about the four 'race' items for Thursday – I would like to have been a spectator on that day.

The Magpies, 1913. Chorley's football team started in the 1880s and played on several pitches. It was only in 1920 that they first played in Victory Park, which had become their permanent home.

Chorley, looking north, 1920s. To the left of centre is the 'Flat Iron' market-place with a gas holder on it, several years before the public baths was built in the '30s. In the foreground is St George's Church and beyond it, curving to the left, is Clifford Street. Chorley railway station is to the lower right, still with its canopies and goods yards. Stump Lane Bridge can be seen upper centre, with the railway to Blackburn continuing to the top of the picture. At the nearside of Stump Lane Bridge can be seen Chorley's engine shed, where three or four engines were based. The shed closed in 1922.

Fazackerley Street, *c.* 1900–10. The top view shows a busy street with many shoppers. It looks as if it is a market day, with the stalls visible in the background. In the distance are many mill chimneys. Below is a similar view in the 1930s. Some of the vehicles are of interest. Dunderdales shop is to the right, and the new Co-op building, opened in 1922 as a footwear branch, is to the left.

Playing in the 'backs' behind Smith Street and Pilling Lane, Chorley, 1930s. Back row, left to right: John Nelson, Ethel Nelson, Joan Lever, Connie Oates, -?-. Front row: Mary Nelson.

Chorley 'Flat Iron', also called the cattle market, mid-1930s. The last sale of animals there was held in the 1930s. The auctioneer in the bowler hat to the left is Mr Lee, with his assistants also in bowlers. Mr Tom Scott, assistant auctioneer, is to the right of the three.

Chorley fair, when the steam-driven 'Gallopers' was a popular ride, 1920s. The travelling fair has, until recent years, had its home on the 'Flat Iron' market-place. Sadly, the era of the travelling fair in Chorley seems to be coming to an end, squeezed out because sites are no longer available.

The half-demolished building is the old Royal Oak, which stood opposite the present Town Hall. This view, taken in 1938, shows just how narrow Market Street was at that time. The Odeon Cinema, which was built on part of the Oak yard, was opened in 1937.

An air raid shelter, 1939. Built at the end of Union Street close to the parish church, this was a demonstration model of how 'domestic' Anderson shelters should be built.

Ethel Nelson from Chorley in 1947, wearing clothing typical of the fashion at that time.

A group of ladies from the Leyland and Chorley area posing on a vehicle chassis at Leyland Motor Works, 1942. Mrs Betty Sharples (née Mosscrop) from Chorley is in the back row, second from left.

Usherettes from the Plaza, 1940s. In the 1950s Chorley had six cinemas: the Empire, the Royal, the Pavilion, the Hippodrome, the Plaza and the Odeon. The latter two were always regarded by my generation as 'posh'.

A full complement of staff from the Plaza Cinema, ranging from doorman to projectionist, 1940s.

These cottages were located in Back Mount and were one up, one down only. The three families living there shared a common yard and toilet. The cottages survived into the 1950s. The right-hand window can be seen next to the pub in the photograph below.

This small pub in Back Mount was called the Red Lion Tap, usually shortened to the Tap. It was across a courtyard from the main Red Lion, or 'front house' as it was nicknamed.

Cottages in Lyons Lane, 1957. The tall building behind is Timothy Lightoller's cotton mill. Herbert, Timothy's grandson, also lived in Chorley and was the officer on the *Titanic* who insisted on 'women and children first'. The wall to the right is part of the Castle Inn.

Mealhouse Lane, with the old police station in the distance, mid-1950s. There are many memories here as the school dentist was in the building just past the Back Mount junction on the right.

Church Brow, 1940s. This steep hill was part of the former main road through the town. At the bottom of the hill flowed the River Chor through Chorley Bottoms. In the days of the stagecoach this stretch of road must have been hard work for the horses. On the right is an embankment which was made in the 1820s, cutting through the Astley Hall estate. This became Park Road and meant that traffic going north avoided the steep Church Brow.

Weavers' cottages from the early nineteenth century were located at several places in Chorley. These were at the junction of Harpers Lane and Eaves Lane and had large loomshops underneath the living-rooms.

Church Walking Day in the coronation year of 1953, hence the bunting and flags. The children leading this procession are from St Peter's Church.

The 1950s must have been the decade of the coach outing. Here, the residents from Seymour and Longton Streets have organized a trip to the Blackpool illuminations. The rise in fuel prices during that time saw a decline for many years in coach trips for groups like this one. Today, however, coaches are becoming more popular again.

The demise of Church Brow. In the early 1960s the historical road through the town for many centuries was lost, with the closure of Church Brow in order to widen Park Road.

Looking across to Chapel Street, framed by the arch at the bottom of Mount Pleasant leading to St Mary's Church, when traffic was still using the street to 'Turn South Only' towards Bolton and Manchester and so forth.

Spectators are about to move away from their vantage place near to Chorley parish church after this Walking Day procession in the early 1960s. No doubt they discussed the merits of and the clothes worn by the children from all the different churches participating.

Another coach outing is about to take place in the early 1960s. Here a group of local pensioners are in front of St George's Street baptist chapel. My aunt, Grace Nixon of Clifford Street, is second from the left.

These children, whose parents were employed at the Royal Ordnance Factory in Chorley, have assembled at the 'Flat Iron' before setting off on their annual outing to the seaside. Blackpool was always a favourite place to visit, being less than one hour's travelling time away.

Today the buses themselves are also of interest, for the centre one is a Leyland 'Royal Tiger', used on express coach services. It would be a collector's item now. The two outer buses were part of a fleet of perhaps some forty buses which were used to ferry ROF employees to and from work, bringing people from all over the county. During the Second World War some 40,000 people were employed at this large munitions factory.

Chorley railway station, *c.* 1960. Well known to train users (there were no commuters then), porter Mr Bob Mason poses alongside a 2–6–4 tank engine, a Fairburn type which was built in 1945.

Railway bus, 1908. At the turn of the century the Lancashire and Yorkshire Railway Company, who had stations at Chorley and Bamber Bridge (6 miles to the north), had introduced a bus service to run between the two stations, to serve the 'in between' communities.

The canal boat outing is perhaps another specifically local function. The canal passed through several parishes and Chorley itself. The trip was organized by many groups, including Sunday schools. A favourite place to go was Red Rock at Haigh, about 5 or 6 miles from Chorley.

Church Lads' Brigade from Chorley Parish Church passing the old police station in St Thomas's Road, late 1950s or early '60s. Two stalwarts of the CLB in Chorley, Mr Gray and 'Doc' Bond, are on the right. The lads in the band are my contemporaries and are too numerous to name here.

Water Street, c. 1885. The old cottages to the left were demolished in about 1910. The former entrance to Astley Park was in this area, before Park Road was built.

An etching of Duxbury Hall, the former home of the Standish family, as it was in the nineteenth century. It was demolished in the 1950s.

Higher Burgh Hall, the home of the Chadwick family in the eighteenth century. It was a later rebuild of a hall that had been established there some two hundred years earlier. The hall has now been demolished.

Fishing at Botany, 1960s. The railway viaduct in the distance carried the Wigan via Chorley to Blackburn railway over the valley and was blown up in 1968, its ninety-ninth year. This was a popular place to fish, especially if you happened to be a train-spotter. The canal, originally the Lancaster Canal, was constructed through Chorley in 1790. From 1816 it became the Leeds to Liverpool Canal. The M61 now runs to the left of the picture. The mill chimney in the distance belongs to Widdow's, the canal mill. The mill building is still in use, but no longer for the cotton industry.

Botany Bay, Chorley, viewed from the old road bridge. This has now been replaced with a new bridge which caused the demolition of the old warehouse to the left. Botany Bay was a busy place at the turn of the century with many men working there. A short distance away, beyond the house in the centre, was a row of cottages where the workmen and their families lived. The area itself was self-contained, with shops and numerous pubs, where fights were commonplace.

A view of a local street, with workers who look as if they are coming home from work. The ladies are wearing clogs and shawls, the traditional Lancashire dress of a hundred years ago.

Talbot Mill, Chorley, built in the early 1900s alongside the canal, where raw materials and coal were unloaded from barges. The mill was the biggest in the country, with a four-storey spinning section and a single-storey weaving shed.

In October 1953 their Royal Highnesses The Duchess of Kent and Princess Alexandra visited Talbot Mill and are seen here in one of the ring spinning rooms with Major Barber-Lomax, chairman of the directors of Talbot Spinning and Weaving Company. Some of the workers presented are in the photograph below.

Some sixteen machine-operators were presented in total, and some of them are in this photograph. They were Mrs Mason, Mrs Warburton, Mrs Whitehead, Miss Seddon, Miss Marsh, Miss Mitchell, Miss Atherton, Miss Brown, Miss Carter, Miss Tootell, Miss McDonald, Miss Clare, Miss Duckers, Miss Cross, Mr Gaskell and Mr Parr.

Astley Hall, Chorley, was built in the sixteenth century and is set in its own park. It was originally the home of the Charnock family. The photograph below is of the entrance hall in the 1930s, showing part of the decorated plaster ceilings for which the hall is famous.

Cottages and Small Lodge at Birkacre, 1950s. Located between Chorley and Coppull is the area known as Birkacre; straddling the River Yarrow it is actually in both parishes. From the thirteenth century some form of industrial work has been going on here, ranging from water corn mills and 'walk mills' to the calico printing and bleach works of the twentieth century. The River Yarrow is dammed upstream to raise the water to feed this lodge, and a headrace that drives a water-wheel close to the cottages, centre left, known as Higher Forge. Off the picture to the left is Big Lodge, which was used for the storage of water for the bleach works processes.

In 1777 Richard Arkwright, who had invented a new water-driven spinning frame, first set up these new machines in a mill built by Richard Chadwick of Burgh Hall. Only two years later, however, the mill and its machines were destroyed by the 'machine-breakers' after a two-day siege, earning Birkacre a place in the history books. In recent years the lodges have been empty; Big Lodge is now refurbished and filled with water, and Small Lodge is to become a partially flooded area providing a wetland habitat for wildlife in the Yarrow Valley Park.

The approach to the works, showing the huge complex of mills and coal mines, c. 1910. Today there is no sign that industry ever existed here; it has all been demolished and cleared away to become an historical trail.

Some of the tambourers from the bleach works, 1920s. In the centre of the back row is Mrs Morris of Coppull, while Mary Ashcroft is second from right in the front row.

This shire horse at Birkacre was one of the many kept by the Birkacre company and used for haulage. In 1922, coinciding with Guild Year, the Lancashire Agricultural Show was held at Preston. This horse won several prizes on the day.

Some of the younger workers at the bleaching works standing by the dam on the River Yarrow.

A large group of children and young ladies, who worked in the finishing department and the 'croft' in the bleach works, c. 1920. Mr Hargreaves, the man standing to the right-hand side, may have been the department's boss. Most of the people seem to be wearing clogs – perhaps there was a clogger's shop on the premises. In the 1870s there were some 800 persons employed in the Birkacre complex, either calico printing or bleaching.

Birkacre colliery steam wagon. Having a mine adjacent to the works made coal availability no problem, but for coal to be moved further away steam wagons were used, superseding the horses. The driver of this wagon is Mr Benison, on the left, with Mr Yates, the fireman/mate, on the right.

Local families cooling off by the River Yarrow after a walk, 1920s. The group includes Maggie Morris, Lily Rudd, Tom Wilson, Nellie Morris and Charlie Howard.

I can hardly leave a section about Chorley without mention of the Tudor Dance Hall, which was converted from the former Hippodrome Cinema and is now a supermarket. It certainly featured highly in the '50s and '60s with my contemporaries. On this particular occasion the dance was a 'ticket only' function: the annual dance of the Corinthians Hockey Team. The team at the time was, left to right (kneeling at the front): Evick Critchley, Jean Benison, Mavis Roberts, Marion Pearce, Sylvia Benison. Other members of the team, also pictured, are Barbara Wilson, Dorothea Calderbank, Marina Bell, Jean Pearson. Gerry Porter and Peter Booth are also in the group.

SECTION TWO

LOWLAND VILLAGES

Anderton, lying some 6 miles or so from Chorley to the south, is mainly a farming community. Two hostelries favoured by travellers on the Chorley/Bolton Road are The Millstone and The Squirrel. Here a suitably refreshed charabanc outing has stopped at one of the hotels.

The railway from Wigan to Blackburn passed through Lower Adlington. Here is the station, called White Bear, looking north-east towards the Chorley to Bolton line which went through the township as well. The station buildings are typical of all those along the length of the line, which closed in the mid-1960s. On the right-hand platform is the stationmaster. Today the small building to the left is all that remains; the rest has been built over.

An old postcard of Adlington market-place. It is hard to believe this is the main A6 trunk road of today. The Chorley road is to the left. To the right is Railway Road which leads from Lower to Higher Adlington, although the Higher is usually omitted.

Morris dancers from Lower Adlington taking a well-earned rest, late 1950s.

As with so many local villages the community is a close one, and the church is the centre of many activities. Here the parishioners of Adlington's St Paul's Church attend their annual dance in the late 1950s.

Carr House, Bretherton. It was here in November 1639 that the astronomer Jeremiah Horrocks first observed the transit of Venus across the face of the Sun. Over the front door is an inscription dated 1613.

Well repairs or digging for a new well in the Bretherton area, c. 1935. On the right is Tommy George Ashcroft with two of his sons. One son is next to him, with the moth-eaten trousers; the other is on the left holding the divining twig.

Haymaking at Norris Farm, Bretherton, 1932. Mr and Mrs Sutton are with their children Peggy, Alice and Jack.

Croston post office. In the early 1900s the post office was run by a Mr and Mrs Rigbye. Mr Rigbye also had another business as builder and joiner in Station Road. The man in the trap on the left is a doctor, and Mrs Rigbye may be one of the ladies in the shop doorway. I wonder who owned the bird in the cage over the door. The shop-front and the postbox look the same today as they did then. What of the postman complete with a bugle? Was this a standard issue at the time, and when was it used?

Adjoining the post office in Croston is Church Street, one of the most photographed streets in the county. At the end is St Michael's and All Angels' Church; to the right is the smithy, and the pump partly hides the base of the cross, now restored.

Outside the works of Mr Rigbye's other business as joiner, builder and wheelwright. The handcarts were used to transport materials to the place of work.

The United Methodist Church, Croston, early 1900s. In the wagonette standing outside is a group of men from the church about to set off on an excursion.

Part of Croston's Church Walking Day procession, locally called 'Coffee Day', c. 1900. The origins of this name may well come from the word feoffment, meaning a gift or grant of a fee. The term may have been applied to the annual granting of land by the squire. The procession is one of the traditions still maintained today.

Hillocks Farm, Croston. The Hillocks is an area close to the church on the south side of the River Yarrow which flows through the village. It is usually approached via Town Bridge, dated 1683, close to Church Street. In the 1920s the Baker family lived at the farm. Here Mr and Mrs Baker are standing with their three daughters Peggy, Nellie and Kitty. The horse was one of those used to pull a float in the 'Coffee Day' procession. The barn at the farm was used to decorate the floats with paper flowers the day before the event.

'Coffee Day' procession passing the police station, 1920s.

Croston's Urban District Council members outside the Grapes Hotel, 1930s. Perhaps meeting at the local would ensure a great deal of talking was done.

Although threshing time was hard work, it was also exciting for a youngster. I was fortunate enough to help out at White House Farm on Chorley Nab. Here the threshing gang is at Bakers Farm, Croston.

Croston Rectory, *c.* 1930. This was partially rebuilt in the mid-1750s and dates from about 1700. A church has existed in the village since the twelfth century, and until 1793 Croston Church was the mother church of the area, including Chorley.

Matt Taylor of Workhouse Farm, Croston, is holding one of the horses pulling a float on a 'Coffee Day' Walk, c. 1960. Reg Cottam and his sister are standing next to him.

The parish church is a pleasing background to the procession just starting off on its way through the village, early 1960s. To the extreme right is Matt Taylor's daughter, June.

Croston bottle works. This smiling group of employees was employed at the works off Station Road, close to the railway station. The works was run by a Liverpool brewery. Green beer bottles arrived loosely in rail wagons and were sorted and crated. The works closed in about 1960. Back row, left to right: Tom Chadwick, Dorothy Dalton, -?-, -?-, Bill Staziker. Front row: Joan Sutton, Jack Trafford, Doreen Singleton.

Cuerden Hall, about 6 miles north of Chorley, was privately owned last by the Towneley-Parker family. Fortunately it was saved from demolition, and is now a Sue Ryder Home. The extensive park is open to the public.

Rutters or Elmhurst Farm, Coppull. Here Mr Tom Rutter is leading two of his horses across the yard.

Station Farm, Coppull, *c.* 1910. This was where the Hart family began their haulage business with horses and carts, most of the business at that time being coal haulage and delivery.

Chapel Lane, Coppull, *c.* 1910. The two gents in the car are Bert Woods and Bill Lilly. The others are unknown, but I can't help speculating about the man in his shirt-sleeves. Was he the mechanic carrying out repairs?

Spendmore Lane, Coppull. This is the main road through the village from Chorley to Wigan. Along its length are several shops, which included, in the 1920s, Rushton's. Here are some of the staff employed there.

Coppull Moor School, 1913. As with so many school photographs of the time, it seems to have been taboo to smile when having your picture taken. This rule only seems to have been relaxed in the 1930s.

No, not St Trinians but the girls of Coppull Council School, 1933. Back row, left to right: -?-, Alma Trafford, Doris Gaskell, Eileen Morris, Milly Babbs, Jenny Ashworth, Madge Moss, Doris Winstanley. Front row: -?-, Annie Mawdesley, Janie Stringfellow, Milly Saunt, Doris Tiggle.

Coppull is on the edge of the Lancashire coalfield and had several collieries within its parish. One of these was Blainscough Hall colliery, which closed down in the 1930s. This group of workers may date from ten or twenty years before that time. The group is believed to be the miners of one shift with their foreman. The lad in the small tub is Bert Dickinson.

Mr Henry Cooper, who worked at one of the local collieries as a blacksmith, c. 1900. Here Mr Cooper looks as if he is ready to tell us what it was like at the pit in the 1870s or so . . .

Two more colliers from Blainscough Hall colliery.

A group of mill girls, Coppull mill. Two large four-storey mills were built in Coppull: Ring Mill in 1906 and Mavis Mill in 1908. Ring and mule spinning were carried out here. Their architecture and machinery were similar to two other mills in Chorley. The ladies at each end of this group are Nellie Greenhalgh to the left and Polly Morrey to the right.

Coppull Ring Mill steam engine, typical of the many hundreds of engines driving mills in Lancashire at the height of the cotton manufacturing era. The engine and its house are spotless. In the foreground are the controls, while on each side of the men can be seen the tandem engine cylinders. In the centre back is the huge flywheel which transmitted the drive from the engine up the rope-race to the line-shaft pulleys in the spinning rooms. The engine was built by J.E. Woods, Bolton, in 1906. It is described as a 'Triple Expansion four cylinder Tandem Engine'. This photograph shows some of the men responsible for the running and maintenance of the engine; one of them (on the right) is Mr Albert Tatlock. Mavis Mill was demolished in the 1970s, but Ring Mill has been given a new lease of life as factory units. Sadly neither of the engines was preserved.

At Trencherfield Mill, at Wigan's 'Mill at The Pier', an engine of the same type as the one shown here can be seen fully restored and running. It is one of the largest preserved mill engines in working order. Wigan is some 6 or 7 miles from Coppull.

A Walking Day in Charnock Richard, c. 1910.

Walking Day in Charnock Richard, c. 1965. On the left of the front row is Marion Unsworth, with Joyce Green on the right-hand side. The children in the front row include Carole Pearson and Susan Unsworth, daughter of Jean Unsworth. Others in the photograph include in the second row, Elizabeth and Lily Unsworth; third row, Vera and Jenny Roscoe.

Park Hall, Charnock Richard, 1920s. Today this view is unrecognizable as the hall has been rebuilt into a large hotel complex. The manor of Charnock was established in the thirteenth century and was known as a 'nest of recusants' by several monarchs because of the number of Catholic families in the area.

Another of the old halls in the area is Buckshaw Hall, Euxton, seen here in the 1880s. It was built in the 1650s by the Robinson family. The hall was privately owned, as a farm, until about 1937, when the hall and land were purchased to build the Royal Ordnance Factory.

Buckshaw Hall farmland, with Bob Critchley from the hall farm operating the horse-drawn binder, early 1930s. Once bound, the sheaves were lifted upright and leant against each other in a cluster of six or eight; these were called stooks, a word not often used today.

Bob Critchley's children, Frank and Jimmy, with their dog Jack standing in front of Buckshaw Hall. The young lady to the left, also with a dog, is their cousin.

Pincock corn mill, Euxton, c. 1900. The mill, which was water-powered, stood on the west side of the bridge crossing the River Yarrow, at the bottom of the hill en route to Charnock Richard. These are some of the men who worked for Mr Ashworth, the owner of the mill.

Armetriding Mill, Euxton, which is further downstream from the one above. Dating from the early eighteenth century this mill has been used for cotton weaving, furniture making and bobbin manufacture. It is usually referred to as the bobbin shop.

In addition to the War Memorial itself in Euxton, a War Memorial Institute was erected. This was opened by HRH The Prince of Wales in July 1921, who is seen here about to shake hands with Tom Watson, whose parents were acquainted with the Anderton family, who lived at Euxton Hall. It is Mrs Anderton who is standing next to Tom as he is being presented to the Prince of Wales.

The Bay Horse pub in Euxton is the setting for this photograph of a cycle race in progress along the A49, the Preston to Wigan road, in the late 1950s or early 1960s.

St Mary's Parish Church, Eccleston, *c.* 1905. From this view it is possible to see the size of the graveyard, which was surrounded by a wall.

Dole Cottage, Eccleston. In the early years of this century this was the home and cobbler's workshop of the Bretherton family. Here Mr Bretherton and his son are standing with old Mr Edmund Wane, who also had a cobbler's shop in the village. Mr Alexander James Threllfall, who worked for the Brethertons, is also pictured.

The local MP from 1895 to 1913 was David Alexander, Earl of Crawford and Balcarres, of Haigh Hall, near Wigan. He is seen here outside Hawthorn House, Eccleston, standing by the car. The short gentleman with a bowler hat, to the right, is Mr John Crawshaw who lived at Hawthorn House.

Mr and Mrs Worthington with their daughter May, at Alice Moons Farm, Towngate, Eccleston, *c.* 1915. The 'little girl' still lives at the same house today and confirmed who was in the photograph.

In Eccleston family names like Moon, Threllfall and Wane occur regularly. Here William Henry Moon, a wheelwright, is working at the large family works in Parr Lane. There was also a smithy here, a joiner's shop, a carriage shop, a wheelwright's, and other associated jobs for carriage making.

Also in Parr Lane was joiner and builder John Wane. He kept a few cows, together with several horses which were necessary for his work. The stable door adjacent to the shippon, pictured here, was widened so that his pregnant mare could get in and out more easily.

Heskin had both collieries and quarries. This is the entrance to a small drift mine in about 1910. The people in the photograph are, from the left, Tom Freeman, David Johnson, ? Christopher and John Johnson. The child in the picture is not known.

Pemberton House colliery, Heskin. This was also known as Basket Pit for fairly obvious reasons. The baskets were hoisted up the shaft and placed on the small trucks. This may well have been the last pit to use baskets.

These brawny lads were employed in the Hurst House Delf Quarry, Heskin, owned by the Marsh family. Much of the stone was used along Blackpool's promenade, but some was used for roofing tiles, as it split easily.

In the Chorley district some four brickworks were in business: at Abbey village, Chorley, Ulnes Walton and at Mawdesley (shown here). There are none today. The Mawdesley Brick and Tile Works, which was operating before 1850, closed before the First World War.

Mawdesley was the centre of the basketmaking industry in Lancashire. In the early years of this century some twenty shops, with associated workshops, were to be found here. Some 300 acres of land were used for the growing of willows, or 'twigs' as they were locally called. Here workers are 'cleaving' ash logs for basket frames. Among them are Robert Cobham, Dick Christopher, Bert Edgar and Will Southworth.

After picking, then boiling, the 'twigs' had the bark removed. This operation was done by hand by the 'twig peelers'. This group of 'peelers' was photographed at Cowleys Works, Bluestone Lane, in the 1920s. This company also 'peeled' for other smaller firms. Jimmy Marsden is at the extreme left.

One of the small businesses in Mawdesley in 1928 was Cobhams in School Lane, which had a workshop to the back, and shop premises to the front. Wages at this time were about £2 a week. Back row, left to right: T. Parker, Robert Moss, Jesse Cobham. Front row: Mrs Sumner, Lily Cobham, Mary Edgar.

Many baskets were sold via the shops but a large number were sent to markets, some local and some further afield. Here a load of baskets are en route to Rufford railway station, with Dick Watchinson (Dick Wack) in charge.

Hand Lane, Mawdesley, c. 1905. The donkey belongs to Lizzie Marsden, on the left of the picture. With her are her two cousins.

Stork Farm, Hunters Brow, Mawdesley, 1900. Mr Hunter is sitting with his daughter Eliza in the farmyard.

Another procession, another village. New Street in Mawdesley is the location of this 1938 photograph. It shows local girls performing a morris dance outside the Red Lion pub. Ruth Harrison, daughter of Mawdesley's blacksmith, is to the right of the centre telegraph pole.

Croston Pageant, 1951. This was part of the Festival of Britain celebrations, and involved a series of Croston-related historical plays. They were performed by groups from other parishes such as Croston, Bretherton, Chorley, Hoole, Hesketh-with-Becconsall, Mawdesley-with-Bispham, Rufford and Tarleton. These brides and bridesmaids are from the Mawdesley group.

The wood yard of Messrs Mayor and Sons. Located in the parish of Ulnes Walton, some 5 miles west of Chorley, the yard has been established for well over a hundred years under the ownership of one family. This crane for lifting tree trunks was hand-operated in the early 1900s.

The late Mr James Robert Mayor. Born in the 1890s, his generation saw great changes in transport, communication and business. Mr Mayor was around the wood yard into his eighty-third year.

Littlewood Hall, Ulnes Walton. This ancient site includes the timber-framed barn shown here. In this photograph members of the local Chorley and District Historical and Archaeological Society are on a visit to the hall barn in the early 1960s. Some of the members here are Mrs Williams, Graham Chadwick, Twells Hull, Tom Crear and Jack Rawlinson.

A class at Charnock Richard School, 1890s. This is another photograph illustrating the very serious faces of the children. The headmaster Mr Ling is at the back, with another teacher on the right.

This photograph, taken at Coulgate Farm, Wrightington, formerly in the parish of Croston, shows relatives of the Harrison family of Mawdesley posing by a haystack. The occasion is unknown, but it is certainly worthy of a second glance.

A local charabanc outing, 1920s. The group may be from the Brinscall/Wheelton area. Perhaps they are on their way to the local hill country.

SECTION THREE

HILL COUNTRY

White Coppice, Anglezarke, 1930s. This gang of Liverpool Corporation waterworks men was working in the 'goit', a watercourse which links the reservoirs at Abbey village with those of Rivington. John Southworth is on the right at the front.

Albert Ephraim Eccles of White Coppice. A temperance reformer who was described in a Directory of 1890 as 'Cotton Manufacturer, White Coppice Mill, living at Albion Villa', he was known throughout the country for his work with the temperance movement.

Brinscall men working by the 'goit', 1948. Although the same length of water as on the previous page, this view is a little more upstream, nearer to Brinscall. William (Bill) Jackson is on the left, with Jimmy (Pop) Brindle on the right.

Yew Tree Inn, Anglezarke, mid-1930s. Although the parish is very spread out, with small groups of cottages and farms, there is a local pub. Here the local hunt is about to set off.

White Coppice cricket team, 1957. Here the captain, Mr Norval Smith, is presented with the Chorley and District Amateur League Cup by Mr Griffiths. Others in the photograph, from left to right, are -?-, -?-, Walter Smethurst, Harold Livesey, T. Atherton, Jim Woodcock, Alan Critchley, Bill Holden, Harry Howard, Donald Gregson, Ken Sowerbutts, and Bill Farnworth.

Heapey railway station, on the Chorley to Blackburn line. It was a favourite place for walkers and hikers to de-train, being close to White Coppice for picnics and walks over the adjoining moorlands. For many years the stationmaster at Heapey was Mr Makinson, seen here.

A Blackburn-bound train at Heapey station. The goods shed on the far right was used for the storage of materials, such as wood pulp, which were waiting for onward road transportation to Withnell Fold paper mill. Raw materials and finished goods in and out of Heapey bleach works were also served by this station; a private rail line ran to the works from beyond the signal-box.

At White Coppice again, *c.* 1900. This time we are on the Heapey side of Warth Brook, the cricket pitch being in Anglezarke. Warth Farm is on the right and the school is in the distance. This was used for weekday and Sunday school. Perhaps the two lads and donkey cart have been to the station to collect a few things.

Coronation Festival, 1953. The parish church in Heapey is but a short distance from Lower Wheelton, and events were often shared. This is the float for the Heapey and Wheelton Coronation Festival Queen.

Rivington reservoirs, constructed in the 1850s to supply Liverpool with drinking water. The natural beauty of this part of the West Pennine moors is enhanced by the large stretches of water. This view is taken from a painting by Hulme.

Old Rachels Farm, Rivington, 1890s. Rivington has many isolated farms, although a lot of them have long gone and are just a pile of rubble. Old Rachels, pictured here, is one such. Mrs Evans with her children is standing in front of the farmhouse.

Black-a-Moors Head, Rivington village. On the right stands the pub which was usually referred to as 'Black Lad'. The pub was moved from its original location when the reservoirs were built. The building shown here was demolished in 1903.

Liverpool Corporation bought much of the land around Rivington in order to construct the reservoirs, but the manor and hall of Rivington were saved. In 1898 this was bought by Mr W.H. Lever, the soap manufacturer, who was later to found the Port Sunlight works and town. A large garden was constructed on the steep hillside and a wooden bungalow was built by Mr Lever.

Lord Leverhulme was a great public benefactor and an important industrialist. Because of this his wooden bungalow (see p. 101) was targeted by the women's suffragette movement to publicize their cause. On 8 July 1913 the bungalow was set alight by one of the local suffrage groups. However, it was not long before another bungalow, this time built from stone, arose from the ashes. To the right of it stands Headless Cross, which was later returned to its original location in Anderton village.

Hall Barn, Rivington, is thought to date back to Saxon times, having six pairs of massive oak cruck frames. Refurbished, with new aisles added in the early 1900s, it still has a full and active role, a venue for parties and dances throughout the year, or just a place to call into for a cup of tea during the daytime.

Rivington Hall was rebuilt in the 1780s. The first hall on the site was built in about 1478.

The back of Rivington Hall, which still has its random stone construction and datestones of 1713 and 1732. This photograph shows some of the staff who worked at the hall in the 1890s.

Hall Barn, Rivington, 1918. These people are attending a retirement presentation for the Revd Mr Ritson, Vicar of Rivington parish church for many years. He is in the centre of the photograph. To his left is Mr W.H. Lever, now Lord Leverhulme, who had much improved the Rivington estates with the refurbishment of Hall Barn and Great House Barn, the building of a replica of the ruined Liverpool Castle, and the laying out of the bungalow grounds, now containing a zoo, and many other works. Next to Lord Leverhulme is the wife of Mr Ritson.

Rivington parish churchyard. A large number of stones, allegedly from demolished buildings in the area, are placed in this churchyard. The Anderton Stone, seen here, is one of those whose origins are lost. Local historian and friend, the late Jack Rawlinson, is examining the stone.

Just to the north of Chorley is the Sea View pub, as popular today as when this picture was taken in the early years of this century. The timber-frame decoration is of stucco only, but eyecatching. Today it has a frontage in its original stone. The name of the landlord at the time is of interest!

Across the road from the Sea View pub is a Georgian mansion called Waterloo Lodge. During the early years of this century up until the 1920s the house was used by many organizations for conferences and meetings. Here a group of attendees pose at the rear of the building.

Haymaking, Kanes Farm, Whittle le Woods, 1919. Typical of so many of the former rural areas shown on old photographs, the land which yielded this crop of hay is now built over.

ROF Gala Day, 1938. Chorley Royal Ordnance Factory was built between 1937 and 1940. To celebrate the huge amount of progress made over one year, a Gala Day was held on an adjacent playing field. The guest of honour was the popular 'Lassie from Lancashire' Gracie Fields, seen here trying her luck at one of the sideshows.

The coming of the motor car in the early 1900s was not just an interesting event, for some it was a challenge. At least two local men with engineering skills had aspirations to build their own cars, which they did in workshops behind their houses. One of these men was John Silcock of Whittle le Woods, who allegedly got his car push-started by the village constable. But John's vehicle seems to have been a one off.

The other man, however, not only built a car, but set up a production line to build several of them. His name was Jimmy Withnell of Clayton le Woods, whose engineering business had been established since 1891. His cars were known as JWCs (Jimmy Withnell Cars). He also manufactured motor cycles and bicycles. This 1910 photograph, taken outside the home and workshop of Jimmy Withnell, shows an interesting line-up of vehicles. From left to right: a 1904 Humber with passenger Bill Marsden of Eccleston; a 'Stevens' built by JWC; a 'Minerva' built by JWC (driven by Jimmy Withnell himself, with his wife and children in front); a JWC motor cycle; a De Dion Bouton made by JWC; a JWC based on the De Dion.

Jimmy Withnell died of typhoid in 1912, aged forty-two. The business continued for a time under his eldest son Tom, then under his younger son Jim until it closed in 1930.

Johnsons Hillock locks, early 1960s. This flight of locks was constructed to connect the new Leeds to Liverpool Canal to the Lancaster Canal at Whittle Springs Basin, just beyond the lock in the photograph. The footbridge to the right is over the Lancaster Canal itself. The canal is drained for repairs.

A brewery at Whittle Springs supplied ales and stouts throughout the county. Water for brewing was taken from the famous Whittle Springs, which was supposed to enhance its quality. Barrels of beer from the brewery were transferred to the canal wharf, via a tunnel, for loading on to the barges.

Chorley Old Road, Whittle. This was the old turnpike road through the village and many of the stone cottages along this road date from that time. To the right is Rock Villa Road, with a sign at the end over a corner shop.

The corner shop, with Mr and Mrs Hogg, the shopkeepers, standing by the door, c. 1905. On the cart is a Mr Blogg, so I am informed.

Chorley Old Road, Whittle, looking to the north towards the Duke of York pub (to the right of the tree in the distance). A large clog can also be seen jutting out from the wall (see below). To the left are open fields, now built upon.

The clogger's shop, next to the Duke of York pub, c. 1900. The shop was run by Mr J. Beaver, who is second from the left; next to him, in the centre, is Bill King. The poster to the right is advertising 'a knife fight'.

Canal tunnel, Whittle. By the Duke of York pub is a canal basin which had the same name as the pub. To get to the basin, boats coming from Chorley passed along the Lancaster Canal and under the tunnel. The bridge in the distance is next to the pub, with the basin beyond.

Duke of York basin. This view, looking across the basin to the Duke of York pub, shows the bridge mentioned in the previous photograph. The clogger's shop can be seen to the right of the pub. The wharf here was used to load stone and millstones from Whittle Hills quarries and to unload coal and other goods.

Walton Summit, terminus of the Lancaster Canal southern section, some 2 miles north of Whittle. Here barge loads were transferred to a horse-drawn railway for onward movement to Preston, where they were loaded on to barges again. The canal is entering the basin at the bottom left; the three arms of the basin can be seen.

The boatyard of Messrs Crook and Co., Riley Green, Hoghton, at the launching of a wide canal barge in 1953. The yard was on the Leeds to Liverpool Canal, some 4 miles from the locks at Johnsons Hillock.

The south side outer gatehouse of Hoghton Tower, 1950s. This sixteenth-century fortified manor house is set atop a hill with commanding views of the countryside around it. It was here in 1617 that King James I knighted the loin of beef, naming it 'Sir Loin'. Over the centuries it has played host to royalty, the rich and the famous.

A view of Brindle village showing the parish church of St James and the local hostelry, the Cavendish Arms – so-called because of the links that the area has with the Derbyshire family of Cavendish.

Victoria Street, Lower Wheelton, *c.* 1910. Behind the houses was the cotton mill of Peter Todd, who had great regard for his employees, providing houses, shops and so forth in the community. The house on the right-hand side pre-dates the mill cottages. This is a handloom weaver's cottage of eighteenth-century origin.

Cowburn's shop in Lower Wheelton. In the donkey cart is Herbert Cowburn, the butcher's son, with a friend. Herbert ran the shop after 1916 when his father died. Notice the window counter.

Village smithy, Lower Wheelton. The smithy served not only the rural community, but also the industrial firms within the village. In the 1850s there were two blacksmiths in the village, George Heys and Jonathan Tomlinson. From about 1890 there was one only. The photograph shows Jim Gregson, who was the last smith to work the smithy – between 1904 and 1920.

The hill villages to the east of Chorley, while idyllic in summer-time, are frequently cut off by snowfalls in winter. Snow often falls in these areas when there is none in the town. The photograph shows the effect of snow near Abbey village in the early 1960s.

Walking Day, Lower Wheelton. As mentioned earlier, Heapey and Lower Wheelton shared many activities. Here, the Heapey parish church walkers are in Lower Wheelton village.

A view of the canal boats, Wheelton, looking towards Blackburn, 1930s. The Leeds to Liverpool Canal passes through the picturesque countryside of Wheelton. In the foreground is a powered Flyboat pulling three dummy barges (these had no power of their own); all three seem to be 'loaded to the gunnels'.

The Leeds to Liverpool Canal is 127 miles long and was the last trans-Pennine route to be completed, but the first to get the approval of Parliament. It originated in the 1720s when schemes to canalize the River Douglas were approved, allowing goods to be transported from the River Ribble to Wigan. The canal, completed in 1816 as a through route, has almost a hundred locks, two long tunnels of 550 yards and 1,600 yards, and an aqueduct of eight arches over the River Aire.

Class 7 at Brinscall Wesleyan School, *c.* 1920. The teacher to the left is Annetta Reeves, and to the right Elsie Benson.

The Guest family were cloggers in Brinscall village. Here, in the yard behind the shop, is George Guest, standing, with his son Bert sitting down. Behind them is a bench on which a specially mounted chisel roughly shaped the wooden clog soles. Bert later took over the business and had a son called George.

School Lane, Brinscall. The bridge crossing the road carried the railway from Wigan to Blackburn. The painter's, plumber's and furnisher's shop of Cunliffe and Son to the right, and the two adjacent properties, were converted into a cinema in the 1930s. This replaced the wooden hut which had been used as a cinema since 1913. It was run by Jimmy Beaver.

Young ladies from Brinscall in Guide uniform, late 1940s. Back row, left to right: Betty Benson, Dorothy Ford, Annie Walmsley, -?-, Annis Frost. Middle row: Elizabeth Ashworth, Winnie Brown, -?-, Margaret Ashworth, Marjorie Waring. Front row: -?-, -?-.

I was unable to find out exactly where, when and why this large group of people is gathered together at Brinscall. Perhaps some reader may resolve the problem. The location is either Brinscall Hall or Brinscall Lodge.

The traditional pub outing, locally at least, usually meant the use of a coach for the 'do'. This, of course, allowed a copious amount of the local brew to be taken along as well. Here regulars from the Bull's Head, Brinscall, are at Fleetwood in 1952, sampling the beer.

Withnell Brick and Terracotta Company. Not only did the works make ordinary common and hard facing bricks, they also made complicated and ornamental terracotta wares. This material is almost like pottery. Much of the terracotta went into the architectural decoration of cotton mills. Some of the different patterns can be seen in the picture.

Walking Day, Abbey village, 1920s.

South Marl Pits Farm, Wheelton, 1926. At that time the farm was worked by Richard Whalley, seen here with his grandson Jim Whalley. Jim also farmed throughout his life and now lives in retirement a short distance away.

Shearing time, Lower Roddlesworth Farm, Abbey village, early 1950s. Among this busy group are members of the Whalley family: Jim, to the left, and Stuart, in the centre.

'Sermon Sunday' at Withnell Fold. The congregation of the Wesleyan Chapel gathers on the front lawn of Withnell Fold Hall, home of the Parke family, owners of the large paper mill which formed the heart of this small community. Conducting the singing is Mr Wilson. Members of the Parke family are standing to the left.

Withnell Fold village grew with the paper mill, which was established in the 1840s alongside the canal, and had no through road. A close community, its cricket team can be seen here in the 1920s, with guest Leorie Constantine, the famous West Indian cricketer, about to play a benefit game.

A wedding in Brinscall, 1935. Although no one envisaged it at the time, the bride was destined for international acclaim as a singer. Born at Higher Walton village, Kathleen Ferrier attended school at Blackburn. There she became friendly with Florence (Flo) Wilson of Withnell Fold. As a regular visitor to Withnell Fold, Kathleen and Flo's brother Bert began a relationship, and in 1935 got married.

The wedding itself was at Brinscall Methodist Church, the reception was in Withnell Fold and the official photographs were taken at a studio in Chorley. Kathleen studied for the piano, and was an accomplished pianist before starting to sing in the early 1940s. Within a comparatively short time she was singing in opera houses world-wide, such as London and Milan. She was accompanied by the best conductors and her records sold by the thousands.

At least five books have been written about her life, the latest ones were in 1990 (in French) by Payot Lausanne, and in 1992 by Paul Campion. Tragically, at the height of her career, Kathleen became ill and died in the early 1950s. In the photograph, from left to right, are: Flo Wilson, Bill Wilson, Bert Wilson, Kathleen Ferrier, Wynne Ferrier, Bert Ferrier, Trixie Ferrier.

As previously mentioned Withnell Fold was a mill village, growing with the paper mill which started in 1844. In 1944, its centenary year, celebrations were postponed because of the war. It was only in 1953, the coronation year, that a Centenary Celebration Party was held in Blackpool Winter Gardens. The photograph shows employees at Blackpool.

Rivington Pike, viewed across Lower Rivington reservoir, perhaps typifies the hill country in the Chorley area.

Chorley 'Flat Iron' market in the early 1960s. The name may well originate from the late 1860s, when a valley, complete with stream, was on the site known today as the 'Flat Iron'. The stream flowed from the railway station area to Chorley Bottoms where it joined the River Chor. The valley was filled in during the late 1860s. The levelling of the site was often referred to as resembling a flat iron. Possibly from this the name stuck. But the town has been associated with a market from the earliest times, when stalls were erected on Town Green, later in Market Street, where a Market Cross used to stand.

The first official reference to the town having a market is to be found in the sixteenth century, when the right to hold a market was questioned, for it was usual that a market charter was granted by the king, or at the very least by the local lord. During the reign of King Henry VIII, between 1509 and 1547, his 'itinerant surveyor of land' in the kingdom was Leland. He described the town thus: 'Chorle, a wonderfull poore or no market', yet he had called it 'a little market town in Leylandshire'.

The 'Flat Iron' became the town's market-place in the period after the 1870s, although fish stones and a pump were erected on a new market site east of the main street in 1826. Today Chorley is still a market town; the stalls are in the process of being refurbished, and one hopes that the market character of the town will continue unchanged into the twenty-first century.

Chorley had an active Cycling Club from the Victorian years. Many photographs show their varied machines over the years. Here we see some of the members from about 80 years ago, posing at some local beauty spot.

ACKNOWLEDGEMENTS

I would like to thank the following groups, organizations and individuals for permission to use, or the loan of, photographs; also for the numerous anecdotes and information given to me during my research: the early local photographers who left us the images of yesteryear; my lecture audiences throughout the district for donations of photographs; members and friends in Chorley and District Historical and Archaeological Society; the photograph collections of Councillor E. Bell, *Chorley Guardian*, Chorley Central Library, Mrs N. Greenhalgh, Mrs J. Heggie, A. Marsden, the late Mr A. Threlfall; the following individuals: Miss Aspinall, Mrs Bommer, Geoff Bellis, Janie Crook, Norman Entwistle, Twells Hull, Mrs and the late Hubert Kane, Robert Moss, Ruth Marsh, Nellie Mayor, Pauline Nelson, Cliff Owen, Richard Robinson, Mrs Frances Ramsden, Norval Smith, John Smith, Betty Sharples, Flo Scott, Roger Taylor, Jim and Stuart Whalley, Jim Withnell. My thanks also to anyone whom I have inadvertently omitted. This will be corrected in any future editions.